CODY
and His Type 1 Diabetes

Amanda King
Author and Photographer

CODY
and His Type 1 Diabetes

Amanda King
Author and Photographer

Interior Image Credit: Amanda King

Special Thanks to Elm Point Animal Hospital

Archway Publishing books may be ordered through booksellers or by contacting:

Archway Publishing
1663 Liberty Drive
Bloomington, IN 47403
www.archwaypublishing.com
1 (888) 242-5904

ISBN: 978-1-4808-7391-9 (sc)
ISBN: 978-1-4808-7392-6 (e)

Print information available on the last page.

Archway Publishing rev. date: 02/11/2019

Dedicated to my mom who supported me through years of insulin shots, blood sugar checks, infusion site changes, doctor appointments, and life. Love you always!

This is Cody and he does not feel good.

Cody is very thirsty.

Cody is very sleepy.

Cody has to go potty a lot.

4

Cody goes to see the doctor.

The doctor tells Cody that he has type 1 diabetes, but everything is going to be okay.

Cody is feeling scared.

The doctor gives Cody insulin to take
because his body doesn't make it anymore.

Cody must check his blood sugar levels to
see how much insulin to take.

Cody takes his insulin and checks his blood sugar.
He starts to feel better!

Cody can still go to the park.

Cody can still play ball.

Cody can still go for rides in the car.

Cody can still play with his best friend Sammie.

15

The most important thing of all is that Cody is a brave, healthy, and happy puppy and can still have fun!

Dear Parents,

The diagnosis of Diabetes can be scary and overwhelming for all those involved, especially the parents. Parents must immediately learn as much as they can about this new diagnosis, what individual medical necessities their child will need, and how they are going to integrate it into their current lifestyle. To do this parents have unlimited access to books, classes, support groups, and the internet to learn the basics of insulin injections, blood sugar checks, carb counting, sick days, insurance coverage, prescription benefits, medical supply ordering, etc.

What about the confused and scared child who is too young to understand the what and why of Diabetes. They are being admitted to the hospital and being stuck with needles to get blood sugar readings, syringes are being used to injected insulin, and they don't feel good. This is when, *Cody and His Type 1 Diabetes*, becomes a useful and valuable tool. Every newly diagnosed young child will relate to Cody. The book is written in a language that is age and developmentally appropriate which will be calming and give them a better understanding of what and why their life has been forever changed.

Warm Thoughts,
Amanda King

17

Amanda King, was diagnosed with Type 1 Diabetes on September 3, 1993 and currently lives in St. Charles, MO. She was 14 years old when she was diagnosed, and she'll never forget the overwhelming and scared feelings she had as she was being admitted to St. Louis Children's Hospital. If Amanda felt this way at 14 years old, what about those children who are too young to understand the what and why of Diabetes. On her 25th year Diabetes anniversary, she saw the need for a book that explained Diabetes on the appropriate age and developmental level for a young child and decided to fill that need. Amanda hopes this book will help young children gain a better understanding of their new lifestyle in a positive way, so they can live the life they deserve.

Amanda has a graduate degree in Early Childhood Special Education and loves teaching and learning from her students. She believes that reading is one of the most important parts of learning and books are not only educational but can also provide comfort and support.

The lovable main character is Cody an 11-year-old ShihTzu Maltese mix that became a part of the author's family at 8 weeks old. He loves to snuggle, go to the dog park, play ball, and play with his best friend Sammie, 10-year-old cockapoo.

Printed in the United States
By Bookmasters